Platform Papers

Quarterly essays from Currency House

No. 12: April 2007

PLATFORM PAPERS
Quarterly essays from Currency House Inc.
Editor: Dr John Golder, j.golder@unsw.edu.au
Currency House Inc. is a non-profit association and resource centre advocating the role of the performing arts in public life by research, debate and publication.
Postal address: PO Box 2270, Strawberry Hills, NSW 2012, Australia
Email: info@currencyhouse.org.au Tel: (02) 9319 4953
Website: www.currencyhouse.org.au Fax: (02) 9319 3649

ISBN 978 0 9802802-0-3
ISSN 1449-583X

Cover design by Kate Florance
Typeset in 10.5 Arrus BT
Printed by Hyde Park Press, Adelaide

This edition of Platform Papers is supported by donations from the following: the Keir Foundation, Katharine Brisbane, Malcolm Duncan, the Greatorex Foundation, David Marr, Alan Seymour, Mary Vallentine and Jane Westbrook. To them and to all our supporters Currency House extends sincere gratitude.

Contents

AVAILABILITY *Platform Papers*, quarterly essays on the performing arts, is published every January, April, July and October and is available through bookshops or by subscription. For order form, see page 74.

LETTERS Currency House invites readers to submit letters of 400–1,000 words in response to the essays. Letters should be emailed to the Editor at info@currencyhouse.org.au or posted to Currency House at PO Box 2270, Strawberry Hills, NSW 2012, Australia. To be considered for the next issue, the letters must be received by 8 May 2007.

CURRENCY HOUSE For membership details, see our website at: www.currencyhouse.org.au

The author

RICHARD HARRIS has been the Executive Director of the Australian Screen Directors Association since 1998. Prior to this he was the policy and research manager at the Screen Producers Association of Australia. He has also worked at the Australian Film, Television and Radio School and the University of Sydney in a series of publishing, research and curriculum development roles.

During his time at ASDA, Richard has undertaken a number of associated industry projects. In 2006 he was seconded to act as project manager for the newly-formed Australian Screen Council, a body established to provide the film industry with a coherent and united front to Government. Similarly in 2003 he was seconded to coordinate the establishment of the International Affiliation of English-Speaking Directors' Organisations, and ran its secretariat to 2005. In 2003 Richard also helped form, and acted as convener of, the Australian Coalition for Cultural Diversity, a cross-arts alliance specifically formed to deal with trade issues during the US Free Trade Agreement negotiations. Since that time he has represented the ACCD on the liaison committee of the International Coalition of Cultural Diversity, which has been instrumental in the successful lobbying for an international instrument on cultural diversity at UNESCO. Richard has an honours degree in political science from the University of NSW.

Film in the Age of Digital Distribution

The Challenge for Australian Content

RICHARD HARRIS

Author's acknowledgements

Particular thanks go to ASDA President Ray Argall and to Robert Connolly, who looked at drafts of this essay and encouraged me to keep going.

Many have taken time to enlighten me on emerging media issues, but I should mention Dominic Case, David Court, Kim Dalton, Peter Giles, Ross Harley, Malcolm Long, John Maynard, Mark Pesce, Greg Smith, Mike Thornhill, Simon van Wyk and Michael Ward. Rosemary Curtis, Kim Ireland and Drew Macrae at the AFC provided research links, while the ABC's Chris Winter kindly sent me unsolicited research material. Thanks also to the Directors Guild of America, particularly Kathy Garmezy, Jay Roth and Jeff Soroka, who sent me the latest articles and research, and introduced me to Tom Wolzien.

Thanks to ASDA's board and my staff, Anne Bentley, Jeremy Duncan and Katherine Giovenali, who have taken much of the office burden over the last few months.

Special thanks and love go to my partner Gemma Deacon, and my beautiful girls Roxy and Indiana, who gave up much precious quality time with their father over summer so that he could research and write.

Finally, of course, many thanks to my tolerant editor John Golder, who gave a necessary rigour and elegance to the final work.

1
Navigating the hype curve

> The business analyst Gartner some years ago developed the hype curve to measure the advancement of any new technology-driven change. It rises through a 'peak of inflated expectation' before diving down to a 'trough of disillusionment'—easing its way back up a lower rising curve of customer acceptance towards real business maturity. Right now we are in the first of those curves, with the maximum opportunity for confusion.
>
> Michael Gubbins[1]

> [W]ith every moment a world is born and dies. And know that for you with every moment comes death and renewal.
>
> Jalal ad-Din Rumi,
> thirteenth-century Persian poet

Anyone following the 2006 Australian media-ownership debates could be forgiven for believing that the transformation of the media space would have no effect on what Australians actually see on their screens. While commentary raged about important issues such as diversity, competition and new services, the issue of *content*—and in particular *Australian content*—was almost completely absent. It was like the child banished to its room while the adults get on with serious business.

This is despite the fact that the Australian film industry has not only been in decline in recent years, with production levels at critically low levels. Now it faces an extremely uncertain future in the form of a multi-platform media landscape, the focus of much debate, that has the potential to blow apart the industry's established business models.

This is not to say that the Government has been ignoring content. The current review of film-funding measures, for example, promises to introduce much-needed reform of film tax concessions that will, we hope, stimulate much-needed private investment in the sector. This is important, and most welcome. However, as with other film reviews, such as the Gonski Report delivered just ten years ago, in January 1997, the weakness of this current review is that it is focused on an immediate production issue—film financing—that needs to be addressed now. What it will not do is examine the broader structural settings within which the production industry operates, or develop strategies to take account of every aspect of the production-value chain. Yet this is what I believe is required, needed desperately, if the industry is to survive and prosper in the new media environment.

It all boils down to a single question: How are we to ensure that Australian audiences twenty years from now will still be able to access a diverse range of original, quality Australian content on their screens?

As an advocate for Australian directors—I have been

Executive Director of the Australian Screen Directors Association (ASDA) since 1998—I have spent many years grappling with both utopian and apocalyptic claims regarding digital distribution, trying to separate myth from reality in the predicted changes. And, more importantly, what all this change actually means and is likely to mean for the Australian film industry in general and for filmmakers* in particular.

Trying to get a handle on the fast-changing media landscape is a daunting exercise, as new developments occur every day—in internet terms, this essay is already light years out of date—and it is easy to freeze in the face of so much hype and hysteria. That said, I felt it important to put some facts on the table for both filmmakers and policy-makers, and to add my mite to the industry's attempts to navigate the new media's hype curve.

The first task in understanding where we are going is to understand exactly where we are now. What does our industry look like, and how does it work? What are the current settings and established business models? How do the overall structures work, or not work?

My next questions address the realities and myths of the internet. Is the net developing as a commercial entity, or will it once again be found to be a hollow shell? And what is the nature of its challenge to existing media models? Is it like any other technological change, or

---

* I use the term 'filmmaker' deliberately as a catch-all to include anyone involved in the process of generating content, and also to break down the notion that people working in the industry should be expected to only operate in the silos of 'producer' or 'writer' or 'director'. It is also a pitch to reclaim the term 'film' to describe any form of audio-visual production: while it does have some medium-centric baggage, it nonetheless has a copyright meaning, and is therefore in my view richer than terms like 'screen content', which mean nothing outside the industry. In this essay, then, 'film' may refer to any audio-visual work, from a feature film, to a TV series, to an interactive program.

does it present something radically new? If the latter, what does this new paradigm offer to filmmakers?

The other issue with the net, particularly in light of the dot.com crash, is: Where is the money? How do people expect to earn revenue? What challenges are posed by developments such as user-generated content and online piracy? How is production financed, and what are the business models for the future?

I also thought it important to explore the extent to which the net is likely to compete with conventional media, replace them, or somehow merge with them. Will the big players of the old world still be important? Will they simply be replaced? To what extent will it be possible for new players to emerge and filmmakers to go direct to their audiences?

The final question, in the face of all of this change and disruption, is: What should we do? What are the challenges and options confronting us, as we develop policy and industry responses, and how are we to ensure that Australian audiences can continue to access adequate levels of Australian content? What sort of strategy must we put in place to ensure that the film industry is able to negotiate the new media terrain, take advantage of opportunities and face up to the challenges of the new media world.

At this point there are more questions than answers. The most important thing to do at this stage is step back, look at the film industry as a whole, rather than at its discrete silos, and ask serious questions about the future. Where is content likely to be sitting in the new media landscape ten to twenty years from today? And how can we guarantee that the Australian industry has a place reserved at the content table?

2
The certainty principle: analogue's mass trade-off

> We have been trained to see the world through a hit-coloured lens [...] And this doesn't apply just to Hollywood. It's how we assign space on store shelves, fill time slots on television and build radio playlists. It's all about allocating scarce resources to the most 'deserving', which is to say the most popular.
>
> Chris Anderson,
> *The Long Tail* (2006), p. 40

> I'm trying to learn 'movie speak' as fast as I can [...] It's about going to movie boot camp. Why does it cost so much? Why do 90% of the people do nothing for 50% of the time?
>
> Todd Wagner, November 2006

The film business as we know it today is an odd business to be in. At the 2006 SPAA Conference, Todd Wagner, who has recently made the transition from internet entrepreneur to film producer, described it as completely 'bass-ackwards'. Glamorous as it may appear, production is widely recognised as absolutely the wrong end of the audio-visual business to be in. Those who make the real money from content are those who control, distribute and exhibit it, rather than those who make it. One need look no further than the major American studios which, despite appearances, are not really producers in the classic sense, but are primarily in the distribution business (now highly vertically-integrated distribution businesses, of course).

This is not to say that those who make films cannot make money—some make plenty—but from a business perspective this end of the audio-visual chain is seen at best as highly speculative and at worst as a mug's game. Any industry in which the established business model is predicated on 'pre-selling' a large amount of down-stream revenue potential in order to get production funded is not one that makes very much basic business sense.

Under the conventional model, filmmakers' access to screens, and hence to audiences, is restricted by a series of gatekeepers, who have the resources to fund the expensive business of production. So filmmakers spend their time trying to patch together deals in order to enable films be made in the first place. The effect is that these few media players constitute the filmmakers' primary marketplace, something that profoundly affects the sorts of films and programs that are made and ultimately shown to audiences.

So how did we end up in this situation? Isn't content supposed to be king, and those that make it therefore *kingmakers*? The simplest single answer comes down to technology. The communications technologies of the analogue era—with all their costs and physical limitations—have fostered the increasing concentration of the world's distribution and exhibition sectors. Be it the scarce and regulated electromagnetic spectrum of the broadcasting world, the pipes and satellites of pay-TV, or the expensive prints and projectors of theatrical exhibition, potential competitors and new services have faced significant barriers to entry.

This concentration has not only limited the power of audiences, but seriously disadvantaged independent content creators. Filmmakers have limited negotiating power with a big media company. Not only does this mean that they are price-takers, but also that they are disempowered at a creative level. They may not be actually *making* the film, but these media organisations—which have both committed money and also have access to the audience—can insist on high levels of intervention in the creative process (intervention that organisations such as ASDA attempts to restrain, of course). My point is that broadcasters and distributors are rarely simply buying the best ideas and projects from an independent community, but are almost always intimately involved in the selection, development and production of films and programs. Independent filmmakers have little option but to *buy into* this system if they want to both make films and have them seen.

Perhaps the most influential articulation of the limits of the conventional media has been made by Chris Anderson, former editor of *Wired* and author of *The Long Tail.* Anderson's central argument is that the media's analogue era has been based primarily on scarcity, which has had a defining effect on what we have been able to see on our screens. The media have been limited by the constraints of the physical world—space (e.g. shelf space), physics (e.g. spectrum and co-axial cable limits) and time (e.g. limitations of a linear programming schedule)—and these have allowed the dominant media companies to create 'distribution bottlenecks'.[2] In fact, the audio-visual marketplace, which is segmented into time-based units such as screening 'windows' and space-based units such as 'territories', is predicated on these constraints.

The term 'window' refers to the period of time for which a film is available at the various stages of its release. For example, a feature film screens at the cinema for a few weeks, turns up six months later in the video shop, then on pay-TV and finally on free-to-air television. A 'territory' (or 'territories') is the country (or countries) into which a distributor is able to sell for that period of time. Distributors buy the rights to distribute in each country or countries—Australia and New Zealand tend to be regarded as a single territory—and then sell different window rights to the different platforms (i.e. cinema film, video, television film etc.)

The time-based screening schedule of television is another product of technological constraint, which, Anderson argues, guarantees that the majority of content that is produced and screened remains ephemeral: If you don't see it on the Wednesday night at 8.30 pm when it's being screened, it is likely that you'll never see it. Anderson makes the point that it is only television that regards its premium content as so disposable. Much of it is disposable, of course, but not all and not as much as is effectively discarded after being given its brief moment in the sun.

The result is a media system that is too focused around mass markets, and therefore in need of 'big hits'. These 'blockbuster' hits must compensate for the misses, and so must appeal to as broad an audience as possible, rather than being the result of real consumer demand. And audiences have little control: to a very large extent their films are chosen for them by the handful of people who control their cinema screens:

> For too long we've been suffering the lowest common-denominator fare, subjected to summer blockbusters and manufactured pop [...] Why? Economics. Many of our assumptions about popular taste are actually artefacts of poor supply and demand matching.[3]

In Anderson's view, the 'long-tailed' internet world allows these limitations to be overcome, and he calls for the adoption of new business models that will ultimately treat both audiences and creators equally favourably.

A country like Australia, with its small population, is hit doubly hard. In the USA, media concentration has been offset to some degree by its population size and large economy, and the entry of new players and services has allowed the development of niche markets. The cable sector, for example, has developed sufficient audience and revenue over time to create opportunities for people with innovative programming ideas. In Australia, by contrast, the options have remained extremely limited, as we have been unable to develop similar services with the capacity to provide alternative financing. As a result, our cinema and television screens have been filled with imported content that has been bought or rented at prices well below those of production—a practice some might call 'dumping'. Despite shifts in the marketplace and audience behaviour over the past thirty-five years, both of these have remained central.

The introduction of rental video and DVD, for example, briefly disrupted the supply-push paradigm for cinema and, despite concerns about its fragmentation, effects on the market actually created new markets for content. However, the video store is still limited by the amount of shelf space it can allocate to video cassettes and is still tied to the window it is allocated. In other words, while the rental market has certainly provided a glimpse of a more consumer-led future, it remains bound by many of the old world's limitations. Importantly, for filmmakers, while an important means by which to reach audiences, the rental market has not played any part in financing and production, as distributors generally acquire video/DVD distribution rights as part of their 'theatrical' deal, without putting much more cash on the table for the privilege.

By contrast, pay-TV, introduced in Australia in the mid-nineties, has become a financing player for Australian film, largely as a result of Australian content regulations, which oblige pay drama channels to spend at least 10 per cent of their programming budget on Australian programs. It is early days, but while pay-TV has become an important element in the existing financing landscape for feature films and more recently television series—the third series of the hugely popular *Love my Way*, for example, will be screened in 2007 on Showtime Australia—to date it has remained a fairly marginal player overall. Its biggest impact in the near future is likely to be on viewer behaviour, as more people use its digital time-shifting service, and watch what they want when they want, rather than when a fixed schedule dictates.

The international marketplace has extended considerably the arena in which the Australian filmmaker can both buy and sell. However, despite the fact that there is increasing engagement with sales agents, international pre-sales and co-production arrangements, for most producers these do not alter the primary focus, which remains the securing of an Australian free-to-air television presale, or a distribution deal for local theatrical release.

The critical 'mass'

What has worked in favour of the economics of both broadcast television and cinema—though this is more the case for the former than the latter—has been the capacity of these media to deliver mass audiences.

Television, of course, has been without peer as a mass medium. Its pre-eminence as a technology and social form for the past fifty years, its universal availability, and the regulation limiting the number of players, mean that free-to-air channels have been able to virtually guarantee audiences of a certain size. This market power has given broadcasters the capacity to commission the production of expensive content that other services are unable to afford.

Theatrical exhibition, on the other hand, may not guarantee audiences in the same way. Nonetheless, it is the dominant market outside the small screen, and therefore the premium market for the 'social' consumption of content—in other words, the best chance a film has of accessing a mass market. What it offers in addition is an opportunity for the film to either earn 'blue sky' revenues (if it suddenly 'breaks out'), or else, increasingly, to gain marketing profile for the local DVD release or even for the international market (the 'red carpet' effect). In the USA, revenues from the rental and sell-through market, once the secondary market, have overtaken those from the theatrical release, which is now primarily tailored to this 'red carpet' marketing. This is yet to happen to the same extent in Australia, although many Australian films perform better on their secondary releases.

Government intervention

The desire to maximise audiences for content is a strong imperative for the Australian government, which has been a key supporter of the modern Australian industry. Indeed, it is no exaggeration to suggest that without government intervention over the past forty years there would be no Australian film industry to speak of. On a purely commercial level it is easier to justify using taxpayers' money, if there is government support—and there may even be some commercial return on the investment. The capacity to deliver culturally, however, has been an even greater imperative, with the ability of film and broadcast television to link Australians across time and space being a key element in its appeal. Film and television have been important in 'creating' a cultural conversation, a shared experience, and identifiably Australian cultural archetypes, such as Crocodile Dundee or Kath and Kim—what Stuart Cunningham has recently called a 'cultural dividend extracted through cultural regulation'.[4]

It is for this reason that priority has been given to developing interventions for the two pillars of broadcast television and theatrical exhibition, as opposed to technologies such as pay-TV, that have been perceived as 'niche-audience' media. The perception that television and cinema offer the greatest potential to reach mass audiences has remained pretty well unchallenged over the past thirty-five years.

In terms of intervention rationales, television provides the most clear-cut. It is this country's dominant form of mass media; it is watched by Australians of all socio-economic strata; it has access to spectrum which is a scarce public resource; and competition is heavily regulated. All of these create a strong case for content obligations, and over time a matrix of different measures has been developed to ensure that reasonable amounts of Australian content get access to the platform. There are direct and tax-based subsidy measures to assist the production of high-cost Australian programs such as drama, documentaries and children's programs. These are augmented by regulation measures and subsidy provided to public broadcasters in order to ensure that these programs actually make it to the screen.

In cinema, the rationale for intervention is more complex. There is a high level of concentration and integration in the theatrical market, and there are precedents for cinema regulation in countries such as Korea and France. However, there are no government-imposed regulations limiting competition, and the theatrical model is more consumer-driven than broadcast television. So, rather than regulation guaranteeing that we see a certain amount of Australian material on our cinema screens, the focus has been on production subsidy—through both tax concessions such as 10BA, which reached its peak in the 1980s, and more recently through direct assistance provided by film agencies such as the Australian Film Commission (AFC) and the Film Finance Corporation (FFC). For these agencies, the 'mass' potential of theatrical exhibition means that it remains the premier marketplace for feature films, and hence the trigger for their financial support. While they cannot demand that cinemas screen their content, they rely instead on the distributors' demonstrated willingness to take risks by putting up an advance (even if only a relatively small sum) and hope that this will at least give a film a chance of success in this marketplace.

The certainty trade-off

The existing media map, therefore, not only has heavy market concentration, but also a high level of government intervention to address the resulting market distortions. While this combination results in something akin to a perfect storm of anti-creative tendencies, the trade-offs have been widely accepted as critical to the survival and future development of a production industry in Australia.

Ultimately, the issue is one of scale. Concentration in a small market like Australia's has allowed sufficient aggregation of mass audiences across existing platforms to underpin a critical mass of production. Fragmentation, on the other hand, poses a challenge, not only to sustainability but also, arguably, to diversity.[5] Without a small media sector with deep pockets, the options for financing production would appear uncertain at best. If nothing else, what the concentrated Australian media structure has offered—with its privileged access to big cultural audiences—has been a degree of certainty.

It has also fostered the development of a professional production sector. Some filmmakers have formed sustainable production companies, while others have forged careers of sorts making both drama and documentary films in Australia—something that was next to impossible before 1970. Others have built up bodies of work that have allowed them to work overseas. The return on investment in talent over the past thirty years has been nothing less than extraordinary.

Australian creative talent is now widely acknowledged and our film crews are recognised as some of the most skilled workforces in the world. This, together with the rise of companies at the cutting edge of post-production, effects and animation, has succeeded in attracting large-budget productions from overseas. The value of film production work brought to Australia by directors alone is not easily calculated—think of the animation work on George Miller's *Happy Feet*, the conventional live-action work on Baz Luhrmann's *Moulin Rouge* or P.J. Hogan's *Peter Pan*—or the value of the post-production work brought by directors who shoot overseas and then return home to edit and mix. But it must be in the order of hundreds of millions of dollars, no bad return on government investment in the creative sector.

Over the years, these filmmakers have learned to work within a production landscape that, for all its faults, has somehow worked, and in which the rules have, at the very least, become set and predictable. Professional industry standards have been created, protocols established, and relationships developed. No less importantly, this system has on the whole been successful in terms of what it has delivered to Australian audiences, and has represented a good return to the Australian government, which has been such a major contributor to both its renewal and its ongoing development. Prior to 1970, hearing an Australian voice on the screen was no everyday occurrence. Now, however, we accept it as an inevitable feature of the cultural fabric. Today, it is unusual *not* to hear an Australian voice; we have come to expect it.

This is not a wholly successful story, however. The current structure remains structurally flawed, with distribution bottlenecks of the conventional media constraining the development of a content production sector that is both viable and profitable. Australia is not alone, of course: we have adopted an international paradigm that focuses on production, but has no real incentives or rewards for success. However, it is a structure that, for all of its pitfalls and problems, too many filmmakers and producers have been willing to work with, for the simple reason that they now have a stake in its certainty and known-ness.

The question is whether the development of new digital technologies, particularly the internet, offers a means of breaking open these distribution bottlenecks in such a way as not to pull down the Australian industry—which is fragile and vulnerable—with its process of creative destruction. As Andrew Urban asks, will the wave of the digital revolution 'sweep the filmmakers to exciting new shores of opportunity or drown them as it breaks over them like a deadly rip curl?'[6]

3
Entering the world of the long tail

> [T]he great thing about broadcast is that it can bring one show to millions of people with unmatchable efficiency. But it can't do the opposite—bring a million shows to one person each. Yet that is what the Internet does so well.
>
> Chris Anderson,
> *The Long Tail* (2006), p. 5

> [T]here is a big threat brewing, and that's the content side of the internet, which, even without current growth rates continuing, could easily have advertising as large as all television in ten years [...] that would sop up more than half the incremental growth of conventional media, including TV and Cable advertising.
>
> Tom Wolzien,
> April 2006[7]

In 1998, William Kennard, Chair of the US Federal Communications Commission, noted that the conversion to digital technology was a 'truly transforming event of our times'.[8] It is a global event and, like all others, Australian media players are engaged in the transition process. According to Wayne Jackson of PricewaterhouseCoopers (PwC), just about 'every segment of the entertainment and media industry is shifting from physical distribution to digital distribution of content'.[9]

From the filmmaker's perspective, this 'transforming event' has not been limited to the way that consumers receive media: it has had an impact on every aspect of their profession, from development to production, to post-production and through to distribution. We're all digital now.

In Australia, the move to terrestrial free-to-air digital television is perhaps the biggest and most politically-charged shift, with 2012 currently scheduled as the year in which all analogue television signals will be shut down. However, other services such as pay-TV have also been migrating subscribers to a new digital platform, allowing greater interactivity and greater capacity to order programs on demand, while the video rental and retail markets are now almost entirely DVD-based. The other major player, cinema, also has plans to move their cinemas to digital, a transition more advanced in other Western countries, and it is likely that a high percentage of all cinemas in Australia will be digital in ten years' time.

The shift to digital for these services may allow new players to enter the market as spectrum is opened up; it may create opportunities for more channels; it may also give consumers greater opportunities for interactivity and time-shifting, which will certainly change the relationship of the viewer to the advertiser, and interrupt the business models of the current media sector. The shift to the digital technologies of the internet, however, threatens not simply to interrupt these business models, but to turn them over altogether.

For the first five years of the new millennium the internet was not perceived as a realistic threat to the existing media players involved in audio-visual—certainly not in the short term. As PwC's Matthew Liebmann has observed, the 'buzzword of convergence [...] was readily bandied around in the first dot.com era five or six years ago and then disappeared because people's imaginations were ahead of where the technology was'.[10] While Hollywood and others could sit back smugly and watch the smaller music files get downloaded and shared across the new global medium, the compression and distribution of video files was seen as another matter. The major concern has been to limit the potential piracy threat of this new medium, rather than to see it as a viable business model, and hence a competitor, for the future. All the signs are that this is about to change.

How soon is now?

I have a feeling that in thirty years' time, people writing about the new media landscape will look back at 2006 as a watershed year, as possibly the beginning of the end—the year in which the digital revolution finally arrived.[11]

In headline terms, 2006 will be remembered as the year in which Google created Google Video, then bought YouTube for US$1.65 billion, and Rupert Murdoch bought MySpace. In Australia, it was the year in which ReelTime launched the country's first internet protocol television service. It was also the year in which the large American networks responded to the internet by making episodes of popular drama series available online for download: episodes of *OC* and *Jericho*, for example, were made available 24 hours after being screened; *CSI* was sold on Google Video and *Lost* on iTunes. As Brooks Barnes wrote, with appropriate hyperbole, in the *Wall Street Journal* on 1 August that year, the decisions to sell these series online were 'the equivalent of sonic booms in the media industry'.

And what has led us to this tipping point of sorts? Once again, it is technology—in particular, broadband penetration, which over the past two years has reached the kind of critical mass that will allow the overall economics of the online world to start to add up. PwC research estimates that by the end of 2005 broadband had reached no fewer than 194 million households worldwide. This may still be well short of television, which is in more than one billion households, but it is growing rapidly and is closing on pay-TV, a much more established service, yet which is present in only 330 million households across the globe. The overall penetration of the internet is 265 million (17% of households), a figure that is likely to rise as broadband extends further and its costs decline.

According to Australian Bureau of Statistics figures for 2005–06, 60% of Australian households had internet access, while almost 50% of these were on broadband connection. This represents a doubling of the previous year's figure. So, while Australia may still lag behind other OECD countries in terms of its broadband capacity, it is clear that once the technology becomes available Australians will be ready and willing to take it up. It is this type of growth that is currently fuelling the internet sector, and suggesting that its time may have finally arrived.

The result has been that in a very short period most of the technologies that are expected to make a difference—such as downloading and streaming—are now tried and tested and, as Michael Gubbins notes, have lost their 'disruptive status'.[12]

Heading for the stratosphere?

The arrival of a critical mass of broadband penetration has resulted in the posting of some quite extraordinary figures for the internet. Combine this with evidence of the emergence of some realistic internet business models, and, unsurprisingly, there are similarly bullish projections about it being the engine of growth for the global media and entertainment industries over the next five years, if not longer.

While media and entertainment stagnated worldwide over the first five years of the century, most analysts agree that they are set for significant expansion over the next five at least, riding on the back of the digital revolution. The signals could already be seen in the 2005 figures, where, for example in the US, internet usage had reached 60% and internet-advertising growth outstripped broadcasting-ad growth, posting a 41.2% rise—off a relatively low base, admittedly—compared to television's meagre 4.2%.[13] Most analysts seem to believe that this is just the start.

The PwC global outlook report for 2006 predicts that the entertainment and media sector will continue to be led by online growth over the next five years. Its projection is that the global sector will increase from

US$1.33 trillion in 2005 to US$1.83 trillion in 2010. While this represents a compound annual growth of 6.6%, it projects that internet revenues will be one of the biggest engines, with a growth rate of 12.9% over that five-year period.

Overall, according to PwC, the industry 'is well into a recovery pattern with increases during the past two years exceeding growth during 2001-2003'. Globally, advertising spend is expected to grow from US$383 billion in 2005 to US$521 billion in 2010, with all advertising categories set to enjoy modest growth. However, internet advertising is expected to see the biggest surge over the same five-year period—at a compound rate of 18.1%—from an estimated US$22.4 billion in 2005 to US$51.6 billion in 2010.

And it is anticipated that this growth will impact on the market for content. The development of iTunes, Amazon Google, MySpace, Yahoo! and AOL are expected to create significant outlets for content. Consider television series, for example; digital downloads now make up 1% of the television acquisition market (only a very small percentage at this stage, perhaps). But it is worth noting that that represents an increase of 255% since 2005. By 2007, they are expected to constitute between 10 and 12% of the market—something like a 1,000% increase from 2006.[14]

In Europe, a similar story is unfolding. In October 2006, the respected screen business journal *Screen Digest* predicted that by 2010 digital delivery of movies over the net will account for 8.6% of total European in-home movie spending: 'This represents a 30-fold increase in the value of this new distribution channel.'[15] In 2007 it accounted for just 0.3%.

In Australia in the meantime, while the PwC report suggests that there will be an overall increase of 7% in the overall media and entertainment sector (from US$21.1 billion in 2005 to US$29.5 billion by 2010), the internet business is once again predicted to be the standout success, and is expected to grow by 19.2% (from US$2.2 billion to US$5.2 billion).

Australians are already comfortable with accessing content on the net, even if this is mostly pirated material. As Brian Seth Hurst recently pointed out, at an industry conference in Sweden:

> Shows such as *Lost* and *Desperate Housewives* have faced most pirating, not from the Far East or Russia but in the UK and Australia, where within half an hour they are whizzed around the globe via file-sharing devices.[16]

Perhaps Steve Allen, head of media consultants, Fusion Strategy, summed it up best when he said that 'the minute we get the next stage of true broadband [in Australia] this will become more of a case, not of how many people [download content] but how often they do it'.[17]

So what's different?

So, it looks as though the emergence of the internet as a serious competitor to conventional media forms is already well and truly under way. The question is: Why is the internet challenge any different from that posed by other forms of technology?

The video recorder is a case in point. Audience fragmentation has always been the greatest fear of those with a stake in the media industries. In 1985, the legendary American President of the Motion Picture Association, Jack Valenti, concerned about the impact of the video recorder, gave an extraordinary testimony to a US House of Representatives committee stating that 'the VCR is to the American film producer and the American public as the Boston Strangler is to the woman home alone'.[18] He went on to call the VCR an 'avalanche' and a 'tidal wave' that would make the film industry 'bleed and bleed and haemorrhage'. This is very much the way in which many today talk about the impact of the internet. As we have seen, the content sector and the media industries responded to the development of the VCR, to the point in the USA that it has now become a lucrative market.

Chris Anderson's argument is that the challenge of the digital revolution is more than one of fragmentation in the conventional sense. The internet does not just add another window to the established sequence of releasing, for example. It has the potential to undermine the very fundamentals of the conventional business models for the production and distribution of media content.

Lessons from the long tail

> A long tail is just culture unfiltered by economic scarcity.
>
> Chris Anderson,
> *The Long Tail* (2006), p. 53

Chris Anderson has become an influential contributor to debates about the impact of the internet. A number of articles he wrote for *Wired*, the digital magazine he once edited, have recently been republished in monograph form, as *The Long Tail*. Anderson makes some ambitious claims about the impact of the net on both the economy and also models of economics, claims that will take some testing.[19] Nonetheless, it is hard to dispute his basic argument regarding the *difference* between the internet and other recent technological developments, and the impact that it is having, and will continue to have, on all industries—the film and entertainment industries, in particular.

In summary, *The Long Tail* explains the ongoing economic life a product can have when the current physical and time limitations associated with distribution are overcome. Anderson compares a store like Wal-Mart which, no matter how extensive its physical store space, can only display a limited amount of stock for its customers—and must therefore make decisions about priorities, and stock those products which it believes will sell. It operates according to the law that 20% of any product generates 80% of the business. So, Wal-Mart, faced with limited space, stocks only the top 20% (in other words, the 'hits' that reside in the short head of the sales graph), and ignores the other 80% out there (that reside in the long tail).

This creates what Anderson calls a 'hit-driven' business. He describes the impact of this as follows:

> Hit-driven economics [...] is a creation of an age in which there just wasn't enough room to carry everything for everybody; not enough shelf space for all the CDs, DVDs, and video games produced; not enough screens to show all the available movies; not enough channels to broadcast all of the TV

> programs; not enough radio waves to play all the music created; and nowhere near enough hours in the day to squeeze everything through any of those slots.[20]

Because its online store is virtual, Amazon, by comparison, can stock many times more products—in theory, infinitely more—than a Wal-Mart. And it can afford to offer not only the products that do 'big' business, but those that make a smaller number of sales at any one time, but which may have an ongoing economic life. For Amazon, it is the aggregate of sales in this long tail that is the key. While producers may not become billionaires thanks to long-tail sales, they may well make enough profit to provide a solid enough business model for whatever enterprise that they are in. A studio may see the long tail as a waste of time, but independent filmmakers may find enough revenue streams there to enable them to continue making films.

What this does for those engaged in filmmaking, according to Anderson, is break down the established barriers of the conventional media world. It is no longer necessary to pass through the gatekeepers to get to a screen; audiences can be accessed directly. This means that filmmakers no longer have always to be 'hit-dominated' and looking for a mass audience, but instead can seek out niche audiences.

In this digital utopia, films should be able to find the audiences that they deserve, rather than those they grab hold of during a small screening window on one of the dominant screening platforms.

The key to the change is the growing power of the

consumers, who find themselves increasingly able to demand what they want, when they want it, and the device on which they want it. This is what is revolutionary. As PwC's Matthew Liebmann points out,

> [W]here the revolution might be sneaking up on us is that, on the back of convergence, consumers have more choice on where they spend their time and money on entertainment and media and they have a voice. They can talk back on social networks and blogs. And what that's doing is allowing people to choose what they want, when they want it, how they want it, and shifting the balance of power between those who own entertainment and media content, and those of us like the Australian public who consume it. Australians no longer have to compromise when it comes to entertainment media, and that is pretty revolutionary.[21]

This consumer-driven revolution throws into question all the structures that have been put in place to serve the current system. For instance, time-based economic units such as release windows become less relevant, as consumers demand to watch the films they want, at such times as suit them—not when someone else deigns to release them for viewing; space-based territories slowly disappear, as people begin to access content more globally via online distributors, rather than wait for them to turn up on their local cinema screens.

Is it any wonder that *Time* magazine's 2006 person of the year was 'You'!

4
Show me the money

> If your work becomes enormously popular, making money from that popularity should not be an enormous intellectual leap. OK, you won't be selling people bits [...] People don't buy *bits* anymore, they buy *experiences*.
>
> Mark Pesce, 2005[22]

One of the great dilemmas of the internet to date has been the relationship between, on the one hand, the users' insatiable demand for content and, on the other, their unwillingness to pay for it. While consumers have shown a preparedness to pay, and handsomely, for technology, be it iPods or plasma screens, many of them expect content to be free.

Since the dot.com crash in 2000, the issue of 'monetising' the net has been central to debates about its future. For filmmakers the issue is absolutely crucial. Because even if Anderson is right, and we are indeed entering a wonderful 'long-tailed' digital world in which filmmakers can bypass distributors and find niche markets in which to sell films over time, one question remains unanswered: How will these films be financed in the first place? Jock Given makes the excellent point that just because audiences 'are interested in it doesn't mean that anyone is going to be able to raise the money to do it'.[23]

According to the conventional model, the risk on the expensive production process is underwritten by those who have access to guaranteed audiences. In the new fragmented world, access to audiences is less certain and their willingness to pay far from guaranteed. In the old world, filmmakers went to a few big players with simple, predictable needs and relatively deep pockets. In the new fragmented world, there is a whole raft of smaller players with new ideas and innovative business models. The long-tailed world is potentially exciting, but it is bound to be more speculative.

This uncertainty has been magnified by two separate, but related, developments, made possible by the internet's capacity for digital distribution: the rise of user-generated content production and the ease of piracy.

The advent of digital-production technology—I can shoot a film on my mobile phone, or create *machinima* animations using game-engine software—and the arrival of user-video sites have spawned a generation of professional amateurs (pro-ams). On YouTube, Newgrounds, MySpace, and countless other sites people can upload videos of everything and anything: video blogs, music videos, ex-Iraqi dictator executions. There is now a whole generation of people shooting material or creating animations, and making them available to the world. Anderson suggests that there are now millions around the world, 'some with talent and vision', equipped with the filmmaker's tools:

> Don't be surprised if some of the most creative and influential work in the next few decades comes from

> this pro-am class of inspired hobbyists, and not the traditional sources in the commercial world.[24]

So, is this a fad, a threat to professionally-produced material, or something that will simply sit alongside professional content in the same way that amateur blogs co-exist with professional web columnists and writers on other platforms? The immediate problem for the content business is that while YouTube has allowed millions of hours of user-generated content to be put on the web for the benefit of a global audience, no-one has been paid for any of it.

At one level we seem to be witnessing a re-run of the 1990s desktop-publishing debate, when many thought that having access to 150 fonts was enough to make them a designer. While the publishing industry has certainly changed, the concept of the designer as someone with valuable skills—skills that are worth paying for—has been well and truly re-established. My gut feeling is that, just as the desktop-publishing boom did not sound a death knell for the designer, so user-generated web-content does not signal the end for professional filmmakers.

I have little doubt that demand for professional content will remain strong. As Rick Bruner, head of internet search advertising specialist DoubleClick, recently noted, audiences 'are going to want to see more of that stuff [i.e. professionally made entertainment] than they are the amateur stuff'.[25] Because, no matter how you cut it, quality production still costs money. Occasionally films are made that can overcome their miniscule budgets—a *Blair Witch Project*, or an *El Mariachi*—but these are exceptional. There are even web programs such as *RocketBoom*, based on low production costs, and increasingly low-budget documentaries shot on digital video. Yes, it may well be possible to make savings in our production methodologies, but no-one has yet devised a sustainable business model based on consistent no-budget production. Even Chris Anderson admits, '[I]t takes more than a digital camera to produce *CSI*, and [currently] only the economics of mainstream media can support elaborate dramas such as *Lost*.'[26]

The YouTubes will give people the chance to showcase their talent as filmmakers, and those who exhibit talent and skill via these new sites will no doubt be given opportunities to further their talent. These sites will be a proving ground for amateurs, much like Sydney's Tropfest. They will even be used by professionals as a means of promoting their sites and their content—to provide samples of content that can be accessed in full through another portal. In other words, I suspect that the relationship will be one of 'both/and' rather than 'either/or'.

A more fundamental change is taking place in the relationship between the current generation of creators/users and filmed content in general. There is a new generation of digerati who have grown up with the internet and who relate to content in a completely new way. The former clear distinction between the creator and the audience is being broken down. The general internet public are now becoming involved in the development of films;[27] they can read filmmakers' blogs during production, and dissect films or programs after release on fan-chat sites or via SMS. A friend recently told me that his fourteen-year-old son liked a recent film so much that, having seen it, he downloaded a version from the internet, edited it into a short trailer and emailed it to his friends. I'm not sure whether this threatens or enhances the industry.

In many ways, the pro-am movement is merely a subset of what many consider an even bigger issue, piracy. The audio-visual sector has been protected somewhat from the full impact of online piracy, simply because of bandwidth, which has restricted video distribution over the net, which has allowed it to learn from the music experience. The music industry has been hard-hit by illegal downloading, but, after five years of negative growth, has finally begun posting small but significant growth figures. It will be a different industry, one driven by not only online sales rather than physical CDs but also a shift to new economic models. Recent moves suggesting that the industry's business models will have to focus more on *licensing* than *sales* represent a tectonic shift.[28] Despite this, and even though illegal downloading will continue, the sector overall seems positioned for future growth.

As in the case of the music industry, the film sector's responses to piracy have been generally defensive. Litigation against copyright infringements, lobbying for stronger copyright legislation, and the development of 'rights management technologies' have been some of the strategies employed to crack down on the problem. But as most acts of piracy are committed by members of the general public, 'hearts and minds' campaigns have also been employed to better educate/deter them. At the same time, the industry has itself made efforts to minimise opportunities for piracy. A significant strategy here has been 'same-day' global releasing, which has furthered the move to establish a global digital cinema network that can release films via satellite all around the world on a single day. Ironically, it is the speed of technological innovation that constitutes the biggest problem: for every Napster and Kazaar that is shut down, a BitTorrent emerges that is beyond the reach of existing law.

Perhaps the most productive longer-term strategy has been the focus on the development of user-friendly online sources for filmed content. One lesson the film industry has learnt from music is that piracy can be addressed, if not overcome, by providing ease of access and convenience, at the right price. As Brian Seth Hurst points out, online piracy is in part a response to the old world of schedules and top-down broadcasting approaches: 'We are moving to an on-demand age where consumers have little patience for waiting in line for content.'[29] PwC's Matt Liebmann neatly sums this up:

> [I]f those people that own the entertainment and media content don't respond with digital alternatives for people in a way that provides value for money, people take matters into their own hands, and that is piracy. Now [...] there will always be piracy, it's impossible to eradicate it altogether. But we found when those who own content provide it [...], instances of piracy started to decline.[30]

While piracy will remain an issue, it appears that the industry's fear of *online* piracy has dissipated over the past 12 months, and the primary focus has returned to hard-copy (i.e. DVD) pirates in countries such as China. There is clearly increasing confidence in the online safeguards against piracy, and the slowing of DVD sales worldwide means that the savings from electronic distribution make it an increasingly attractive option. 'Our goal is to seek out as many [viable] retail outlets as we can, and put as many titles as we can on those sites', says Peter Levinsohn, President of Fox Digital Media, which has signed deals with many emerging online outlets.[31]

Perhaps it is a sign of the times that many players seen hitherto as 'problems' are signalling a desire to become legitimate. Google, for instance, whose photograph publishing has recently been the object of complaint, has settled the matter and begun to discuss ways of working with the film studios, including offering programs on a pay-per-download basis, and testing free videos that contain ads. Meanwhile, the Google subsidiary, YouTube, is now signing 'content agreements', while the ultimate internet bad boy, BitTorrent, has also indicated that it wants to start playing by the rules. The poachers are becoming the gamekeepers.

Revenue models

So, what key business models are these new distributors looking at to underpin their online enterprises? Where does the revenue come from?

For the established players, the issue is whether these new platforms actually can create revenue for their film libraries, something that remains uncertain. As Merissa Marr says, '[T]he most tantalizing prospect, the distribution of movies over the internet via downloading services, remains distant as a meaningful revenue source.' She points out that the studios' early efforts in the digital world have had little success. Services like CinemaNow and Movielink have barely made a mark and industry executives are sceptical that they will survive. Nonetheless, the studios are rushing to do deals with all manner of new legitimate services.[32]

Advertising has clearly emerged as a significant revenue earner on the net, and a means of dealing with internet users' unwillingness to pay upfront for content. Interestingly, 'video advertising'—typically, a video ad is a 15- or 30-second spot that runs before or during an online video—is growing faster than any other type of internet advertising. While it accounts for only 2.3% of total web ad spending now—an estimated US$385 million in 2006—it is expected to grow at double the rate of the overall ad market in the next four years, rising to US$2.35 billion by 2010, according to eMarketer Inc. Apparently, demand for video ads is so strong that prices are now on a par with those for television: the cost of reaching 1,000 web viewers is about the same as that of a 30-second ad in an autumn-season episode of *Desperate Housewives*.[33] In the words of MySpace.com's Marketing Chief, Shawn Gold, 'Top of mind lately is video advertising'.[34]

Some have questioned whether internet users who have been used to seeing ad-free content will be willing to accept advertising. This will be an issue for YouTube, which has clearly indicated its intention to run ads. However, according to Tracey Scheppach,

Video Innovation Director for ad-buying firm Starcom USA, internet viewers appear willing to accept advertising as long as they get convenience and free content: 'Viewers seem to prefer watching free ad-supported content versus paid content without ads.'[35]

Another problem with ads, as any filmmaker or viewer of the (until recently) ad-free SBS can vouch, is their suitability for the content they accompany. The grotesquely inappropriate juxtaposition of an SBS documentary on Third World poverty interrupted by ad for a fast-food chain will seriously affect the viewing experience. Filmmakers and net distributors will have to negotiate this terrain with sensitivity to ensure that any advertising adequately matches the substance and style of the content on offer.

Internet advertising will shift and morph as people experiment with different styles of ads—top-and-tail ads, embedded ads, watermarks. 'Product placement' will no doubt be used, as will more discrete forms of sponsored programming. In Australia, the setting-up of creative content companies such as Three Drunk Monkeys appears to be setting the scene for the future. TDM has recently signed a joint venture with film distributors Hopscotch to create 'branded entertainment' projects.[36] Branded entertainment—or what Freehand Media's John Gregory calls 'brand-funded entertainment'[37]—is clearly part of the net's new wave.

For media futurist Mark Pesce, advertising liberates content owners from fears of piracy. With advertising embedded, the more content is distributed and seen by different audiences, then theoretically the more money it should make. In the words of Lawrence

Lessig, the more something is shared the more valuable it becomes.[38] It is now all about finding ways to get it out there.

When it comes to paying for content, the greatest obstacle remains the absence of a viable micro-payment system, such as iTunes provides for music. Simon van Wyk of Hot-House assures me that this will be resolved one day, but that it still remains a major issue for current internet video business models.

Subscription and pay-per-view (i.e. pay-per-download) are currently the primary options—sometimes offered as different options by the same provider. Using a subscription service permits access to content on a site for a certain period, much as a subscription to a pay-TV service does. Some services let viewers stream movies for a certain amount of time, others permit downloading. And just like pay-TV, the models for subscription are becoming increasingly tiered. In time these models are likely to only become more tailored and sophisticated.

The clearest success with subscription fees has been in the area of immersive games, such as *World of Warcraft* (an online fantasy role-playing game), and *SecondLife* (a 3-D virtual world). These games, and others like them, are generating quite remarkable subscription fees as millions log in globally to play them on an ongoing basis.

To own content, you must download over the net. Downloading, or 'Downloading to Own', is full and permanent ownership of the file, generally using digital rights management technologies to protect the copyright of the content. For example, in Australia, when you purchase a 'Download to Own It' title from a provider such as ReelTime, you receive three different files of the same movie, one for the PC, another for a Portable Device, and a third that is available to burn to DVD.

The creator's cut

If money can be generated, the first question film-makers ask is: How is the money going to be shared between those who 'create' it and those who 'show' it?

Many see the internet as another platform, for which they should simply be paid an additional licence fee. And the explosion of devices and platforms in recent years has seen producers try to slice their content more and more thinly, in order to take as much advantage as possible. The real question is: What is the 'value' of the each platform and each type of use? It is relatively easy to determine the value of a single broadcast on free-to-air television. However, content can be delivered in many different ways over the internet—streaming, pay-per-view downloading, downloading-to-own—and revenue models may vary. This value-of-online-rights issue remains largely unresolved and will need to be addressed at an industry-wide level over the coming years.

However, to see the internet as simply one more platform is very much like seeing it through the lens of the old-world structures—because it is about finding a single 'licence' payment for internet rights, as one might pay a single one-off fee for any other release on conventional media. What this approach ignores is the fact that the internet has developed innovative revenue models, which could recalibrate the relationship between creators and end-users in the film world. I am thinking particularly of the concept of 'revenue sharing' between producers and distributors, a well-established internet revenue model that could be explored in relation to filmed content.

The idea that filmmakers could earn money on an ongoing basis—whether it is generated from advertising or a share of content sales and downloads—is a radical one. In many ways it flies in the face of fifty years of film financing. Rather than simply being paid a licence fee by Channel X, told to bid one's project goodbye and to go away and make another, the Googles of the world are increasingly offering the option of sharing in the success or failure of one's film.

In terms of financing, a revenue-sharing deal will mean that a filmmaker will probably have to rely more heavily on private investment than on the deep pockets of distributors/exhibitors. An investor may have to speculate, but at least they will know that whatever revenues are generated will ultimately be shared equitably.

It may be early days, and clearly there has to be some shaking-out in the business models, but right now there is the smallest suggestion of a change in the model, just the glimpse of a possible future.

5 Changing platforms

> If one word could describe the media business in 2006 it would be fragmentation [...] But traditional media companies have responded by investing in multiple media platforms to reach this increasingly fragmented audience.
>
> James Rutherford, Executive Vice-President, Veronis Suhler Stevenson

All right, reality check. Yes, the internet is growing fast and, yes, its content business models are emerging. But will it really disrupt the established players?

Let us just look at television. At the 2007 annual meeting of the World Economic Forum in Davos, Bill Gates repeated his regular refrain that television's days are numbered. But before calling for the last rites to be read, we should remember that television is still big—a AUD$3.5 billion-industry in Australia alone—and it is still extremely profitable.

Television broadcasters are also key content entities. Not only do they own a lot of the material that they can exploit in this new media landscape, but television remains the largest single contributor to content production in Australia. While the Australian commercial networks have recently reduced their spend on what they consider expensive, and therefore risky, Australian content, they are likely to remain the major content drivers for the foreseeable future.

A recent UK report predicted that television, which currently supports over 50% of its £5.8 billion sector, will remain the dominant commissioner of audio-visual content over the next ten years.[39] The broadcasting primary rights commissioning market will remain the key market for original programming, and UK broadcasters, who currently account for 95% of UK television commissions, will remain the main buyers. Just as importantly, the primary commission will remain the most important. According to the report, the primary commission currently constitutes about 85% of the income for a program over its lifetime, and despite the rise of the internet, this is likely to remain above 75% in ten years' time. In other words, UK filmmakers should not thumb their noses at the broadcasters just yet.

Furthermore, television is still growing, both in Australia and worldwide. Certainly, it is not growing at anything like the speed of the internet, but it is still growing. Despite escalating rates of downloads, and dramatic shifts in viewer demographics more television is being watched than ever before. Despite its loss of market share, PwC's short-to-medium term prognosis for Australian television is positive. As Matthew Liebmann explains, it remains 'a highly effective way of getting a message out to a mass audience'.[40] The masses may be smaller 'but the ability to deliver them is still scarce and advertisers are still prepared to pay for it'.[41]

Similarly, in Canada conventional media have remained relatively stable, despite the impact of the internet. According to the Coalition of Canadian Audio-Visual Unions, the levels of overall television viewing have stayed the same or have risen over the past five years.[42]

Third, television as a distribution technology currently has a lock on quality. Until new technologies manage to fully overcome the 'last eight feet' problem—referring to the loss of quality in the transference of data from a computer to a television screen—television will remain most people's medium of choice. Peter Grant observes that while video is increasingly migrating to the web, ironically, consumers appear at the same time to be demanding higher picture-quality on television.[43] The advent of digital terrestrial television will allow broadcasters to make further 'quality-based' pitches for Australian eyeballs.

Similarly, television's user-friendliness will make it hard to displace. One consumer study found that viewers will be inclined to watch films and shows on television rather than on their computers, and that technical issues were the deciding factor:

> [T]oday's mainstream buyers do not have the [...] degree of technical knowledge to cope with the complex installation, set-up and troubleshooting that these products often require—and this survey indicates they have no desire to become their own technicians.[44]

Technologically, television remains the most efficient way of distributing content to mass audiences and, according to Canadian consultants Nordicity Group, will remain the dominant distribution system for conventional programming. While new developments such as compression, peer-to-peer file-sharing, and other technologies will keep moving the yardsticks, the internet currently does not rise to the same level of efficiency. Nordicity notes that the cost of internet distribution of television programming is four times that of distribution by coaxial cable or satellite—which is supportable, but hardly favourable.[45]

Nor should the role that television has played historically as an instrument of culture be underestimated. Since its introduction into Australia in September 1956, television has played such a central part in the linking of Australians through time and space that not even the internet's digital revolution will easily dislodge it from our national psyche. As Kim Dalton, head of ABC-TV, stressed at the most recent ASDA conference,

> [I]t is worth re-stating the power of television as a cohering force, as a medium which can offer and in fact deliver a shared experience like no other [...] This isn't just water cooler TV. This is about the power of TV to contribute to a community's shared historical experience.[46]

Similarly, cinema and pay-TV are likely to remain similarly significant players in Australia in the short-to-medium term. The PwC report suggests that pay-TV will continue to exhibit strong growth in Australia over the next five years, as it continues its own transition to digital and increased interactivity and personalisation. Its penetration is expected to hit 31% by 2010, and revenue is expected to increase by 12.7% (to

AUD$2.9 billion). The advertising growth on pay-TV is expected to be second only to that on the internet. The cinema, meanwhile, remains a key social experience for Australians. Cinema box-office has steadily grown over the past decade, reaching AUD$907 million in 2004. A downturn to AUD$817 million in 2005, mirroring similar falls around the world, led to apocalyptic predictions about the future of cinema and even the feature film itself. However, recent figures suggest this downturn may have been an aberration, with box-office increasing to AUD$866.6 million and predictions that box-office growth will remain positive for at least the next five years.[47]

What has changed is the *sort* of film people consume in the respective media. For instance, theatrical exhibition is increasingly dominated by large-screen-release tent-pole films, with international stars and/or visual effects. These are not the films—George Miller's *Happy Feet* notwithstanding—that the market generally allows Australians to make. And the business that once allowed an independent Australian film to build slowly based on word of mouth has all but disappeared. Even in the niche market, where Australian films compete, there are now more films looking for the same number of screens: while a few years ago about 80 niche-market films were released per year, now the figure is closer to 130. Television, meanwhile, has seen a similar programming shift from expensive dramas to 'event' television (live sports, news and reality shows), where broadcasting still has an edge over pay-TV and internet-delivered content.

What is perhaps more significant, in terms of the

overall shape of the media sector, is convergence. The future of television can no longer be seen in isolation from the internet, but as part of an increasingly multi-platform environment. Fragmentation may affect conventional platforms, but media companies are moving to concentrate and aggregate across them. In this new, converging world, companies that once saw themselves as 'broadcasters' or 'studios' or 'distributors' are identifying themselves as 'cross-platform rights managers' that aggregate content and make it available to anyone, anywhere, on any platform.

These cross-platform opportunities have already been exploited by broadcasters. As we have seen, some are using the internet as a new delivery system to exploit old libraries. Others have used it as a secondary platform for new content, piggybacking off television or cinema. AOL, for example, now sells downloads from MTV, Warner Brothers and Nickelodeon, while in Australia Yahoo7 has flagged its intention to make fresh episodes of television shows available at a price, and the ABC makes episodes of *The Chaser's War on Everything* available by Video Podcast.

Some companies focus more on advertising. Moves by CBS to allow free next-day streaming of seven of its prime-time programs are clearly targeted at taking a 'bigger slice of the growing internet advertising pie'.[48] In the meantime, NBC Universal has begun creating specialty internet channels, such as outzoneTV.com (a gay channel); dotcomedy.com (for comedy fans); and brilliantbutcancelled.com (for TV junkies).

Many broadcasters use their cross-platform presence to drive viewers back to the *primary* television release, a strategy that works particularly well with dramas that have complicated plot-lines. It is easy to lose track of a series such as *Lost*, but downloading old episodes from the net allows audiences to catch up and return to television to watch new ones. The net helps in this by facilitating ongoing fan discussions of episodes as they go to air. As Sydney University Honours student Adam Zuchetti found, in his research on television downloaders, 'People who regularly download programs still watch free-to-air in order to discuss the shows [... They] had to come back and see where Australian viewing was up to, so they could contribute to discussions here.'[49]

Companies are also slowly developing stand-alone internet content. At this stage, this is the more speculative end of the content business, particularly for linear-style narrative programming. While games have exploded on the web, immersive games in particular, audiences are not as comfortable watching original web content and there have not been many stand-alone successes: most of the best-known are restricted to low-cost comedy/news/variety shows such as the very popular 3-minute daily videoblog, *Rocketboom*. Ex-Warners executive Jordan Levin warns that low-cost original programming can be problematic because it risks being seen as 'content that wasn't good enough to put on TV'.[50] However, web providers are starting to become more ambitious. Mark Burnett's recent reality program *Treasure Hunt* was one of the first major net-programming experiments—Burnett, the producer of successful reality shows *Survivor* and *The Apprentice*, recently changed his title from 'TV producer' to 'screen content creator'.

One particularly new development has been programming that has taken advantage of cross-media possibilities in the content itself. Perhaps the best-known example is the 'real-life soap', *Big Brother*, that allows audiences to simultaneously access different forms of content on both the net and television, and interact with the program's outcome via mobile-phone text-messaging. However, there have been other Australian experiments, some more conventionally dramatic but no less versatile in design. For example, there was *Fat Cow Motel*, an interactive drama broadcast over 13 weeks in 2003. A love-story and mystery, set in an outback-town motel, it employed a cross-platform approach, offering viewers the opportunity to determine the direction of the drama. Another interactive experiment, but more intentionally educational in purpose, was *Us Mob*, a choose-your-own-adventure series that enabled audiences to be part of the community of four Aboriginal teenagers in Central Australia, play games with them and dictate the course of their narrative.

Cross-platform strategies can be applied to more than regular content, of course: a recent competition for pro-am filmmakers to make a 30-second advert for Doritos chips ('Live the Flavor'), which would air on national US television during the broadcast of the Super Bowl, is a clear illustration of the way the world of advertising has been penetrated. This initiative brought broadcasting, advertising, the net and the YouTube generation together in one place.

Interestingly, some cross-platform innovations have been seen as serious challenges to conventional players—in particular, the day-and-date release paradigm, which has not only been employed to address piracy problems, but also as a marketing strategy. For example, some saw the 'almost' day-and-date international release of CBS-TV series, *Jericho*, as providing promotional opportunities for the show outside the US. Pay-TV had similar success with *Rock Star: Supernova*, the reality show in which contestants compete to sing with a new supergroup. It screened exclusively on pay-TV in Australia, each episode airing just hours after its US screening. According to the *Hollywood Reporter* of 26 September 2006, the series was the highest-rated general entertainment program in Foxtel's 10-year history.

Todd Wagner and Mark Cuban, of 2929 Entertainment, have moved beyond merely collapsing international release dates and begun experimenting with releasing feature films day-and-date on any available platform. 'Full' day-and-date constitutes the most comprehensive threat to the traditional staggered windows release, and some exhibitors have labelled their company the 'Anti-Christ'. 2929 was only able to release in this way because Wagner and Cuban own cinema, pay and internet assets, and were therefore able to avoid an exhibitors' revolt. However, since they forged a partnership with Oscar-winner Steven Soderbergh in 2005, to direct six high-definition films, the approach has gained attention and there are already other similar examples emerging.[51]

Australian director/producer Robert Connolly is considering a similar release for future films. If handled properly, he believes, the day-and-date paradigm could have benefits for all platforms. For instance, audiences who see the film at the cinema might receive a coded ticket giving them access to additional benefits, a free copy of the soundtrack perhaps. Those who receive it via other means would only access these benefits on payment of a premium price. Or perhaps the distributor and cinema could share in non-theatrical revenue for the first six weeks of release. Innovative strategies like these might lead to exhibitors overcoming their initial resistance to the concept.

So where are we going?

Established players are likely to remain in this multiplatform environment. They have libraries, audiences and relationships—all of which will matter, as they attempt to colonise the web. Most important, however, will be their 'brands'. People know CBS, understand the BBC, recognise Channel Nine. Of course, internet brands have quickly become just as powerful. Google, AOL, YouTube, Yahoo, iTunes, Intel, MySpace—have all become recognised players. And all these brands continue to be where the majority of the world's internet users spend their time. NineMSN still attracts the majority of Australian traffic, for example. In a vast internet cloud people still appear to value 'lighthouses'—someone they trust to bring content together in a digestible, understandable and useable format. In other words, while there may well be an increasingly long tail of small internet operators, it is likely that a minority of sites will dominate the majority of the internet's eyeballs. The next big play will be how these internet brands form partnerships with the content brands (NineMSN, Yahoo7, for example) and where different companies try to establish their own online content identities.

The negative side for many filmmakers is that, despite the emancipatory promise of digital distribution, the basic structures may not change very much. There may not be many backers with deep enough pockets, prepared to fund ambitious content with high production values. So, many filmmakers will find the same people financing their projects, according to the rules that they have always observed—except that now they simply want more for their money. Many Australian documentary makers, for instance, already have broadcasters wanting to buy internet rights for little more than the cost of the regular broadcast licence fee. And, in addition, they often want the filmmaker to develop a series of interactive elements (online and DVD) that can sit alongside the linear film—projects with 360-degree applications—once again for little more. The Oliver and Ohlbaum report referred to earlier foresees this extension of the scope of the primary licence as one of the great challenges for the content production sector over the next ten years.

A positive aspect is that at least there will still be companies with finance available, looking to develop and finance quality content. It may not be clear what they will pay, but the 'short head' where blockbusters are made will not disappear. At the same time, a multiplicity of niches will open up in the net's long tail that could provide fruitful markets for Australian content. Filmmakers too will no longer be so limited by their own country's coastline when looking for financiers and sales: the global nature of the internet creates more opportunities to go to the world.

Finally, net-driven innovations such as the development of smaller niche platforms, new revenue models, and flexible release approaches, particularly in the long tail of the net, have the potential to drive positive changes to established film business models and create opportunities for filmmakers to become more entrepreneurial and have greater control over the release of their films.

Perhaps the best that we can hope is that rather than a single dominant model, we end up with two separate paradigms, one based on a more conventional approach, and another that is more flexible and innovative. The ideal scenario would be for filmmakers to be able to move between the two. The structural and policy settings will need to be flexible enough to allow for this and to ensure that filmmakers can take advantage of the emerging opportunities. If not, Australian filmmakers may get little more than a passing glimpse of a tantalising new paradigm.

6
Supporting film in a cross-platform world

> I found [...] a series of quotes that said things like 'the movie business has to reinvent its business model or it will collapse' and 'people are enjoying staying at home more than ever before' and 'Hollywood has lost its creative capabilities and is relying entirely on sequels.' They all sounded like commonly-heard observations. The only problem was that they were all said back in 1948, 1963, and 1976.
>
> Jim Gianopoulos, CEO, Fox Filmed Entertainment

> [I]t's not just providing compelling content but providing compelling experience and part of the experience may be something that extends beyond traditional content.
>
> Steven Canepa, Vice-President, IBM Global Media and Entertainment

So how do we ensure that the Australian film industry is best placed to survive and prosper in this new cross-platform environment? What interventions by government will guarantee Australian audiences access to the quality and diversity of original

Australian content they have come to expect?

The Federal Government's established content strategies will face many challenges in this new media landscape. Content regulation, in particular, will come under extreme pressure. The Government has signalled its intention to change the broadcasting rules in 2012, corresponding with television's analogue signal switch-off. This transition to digital broadcasting will open up additional spectrum, allowing new services such as multi-channelling, and pave the way for new broadcasting entrants. Communications Minister Helen Coonan has made it clear that, after this date, all bets are off.

While it is too early to predict that 2012 will finally be 'the year', speculation about the end of the existing commercial broadcasting oligopoly has undoubtedly moved from 'if' to 'when'. And, as spectrum is freed up for both conventional broadcasting and other services, the pressure will be on to make existing regulations more 'flexible' or be dropped altogether. As Channel Nine owner James Packer recently made abundantly clear, Australian content will be the first casualty of any change to broadcasting's status quo.[52]

The changing media landscape will also provide greater challenges to policy-makers, as the accepted rationales for regulation come into question. What is the role of broadcasting now that people are watching programs on different devices, at different times? How do we regulate television delivered over the internet? How much should we regulate as the media moves from the supply-push to a demand-pull model? And how do we deal with the different regulatory approaches for broadcasting (focused on *content*) and telecommunications (focused on *carriage*) as the two increasingly converge?

Then there is the difficulty of regulating digital technology. Fortunately, policy-makers have some flexibility: while the Australia-US Free Trade Agreement precludes the Government from increasing regulations on conventional media, it did reserve the capacity to develop regulations for future 'interactive video services'—the one small but important concession that the industry won in its FTA campaign. However, retaining flexibility is one thing—determining the most effective forms of regulation is another.

Direct intervention via subsidy will also become less straightforward. For example, the arrival of the internet as a delivery platform throws into question the established definitions of the 'marketplace' which are used to trigger finance, and their focus on 'mass audience' platforms. Today the FFC relies on conventional triggers such as broadcaster pre-sales and distributor advances. Tomorrow's triggers may be less clear, as new platforms develop new business models for content.

And what content shall we be watching in the future? The conventional linear narrative film appears safe for now, despite claims that it is an old-world relic. Be it a stand-alone feature film, or a shorter TV-style comedy series, there continues to be strong demand for stories told in the conventional way. As Gary Hayes told the 2006 Australian Communications and Media Conference, 'People want to be told stories, share stories, be part of a community and have an identity.' Consumers aren't concerned with media format and how content reaches them—they just want content.[53]

Forms of linear narrative will shift and change, however. The current time-based segmentation will be challenged as the market shows preferences for shows of varying duration. Chris Anderson is convinced that we shall see a 'range of more natural lengths of video content that reflect the diversity of human attention spans and content types, not network programming convenience and advertiser priorities'. Anderson believes that people will want shorter material, as that produced for the net shows, and this is in line with new devices such as iPods that allow content 'to be watched in moments snatched between other things'. Demand will shift to 'shorter content for convenience and entertainment, and longer content for substance and satisfaction. But the arbitrary middle will not hold'.[54] While I agree that demand for shorter films will probably increase, it is perhaps a little early to predict future audience preferences with such certainty.

A market for short films would be an exciting development for Australian filmmakers. Australians have been remarkably successful over the years in short film, particularly short animations, culminating recently in one Oscar and two nominations. With the opening up of new platforms, it is these filmmakers who are best placed to take advantage of long-tail possibilities, as they don't need to recoup massive budgets. This old-world craft sector is, somewhat ironically, the most new-world ready.

Similarly, Australian feature films could be well

positioned to benefit. Our film industry has always struggled to build the critical mass of films required to underpin a professional sector. The scarcity of available theatrical screens has discouraged the expansion of film production—as it is, there are concerns that the small number of Australian films released cannibalise each others' markets. Digital distribution could reduce pressure on the theatrical market; some films might not need theatrical release at all.

To sustain this critical mass with more filmmaking, many potential markets are likely to be smaller niche ones and more films will have lower budgets. This will be offset by the fact that niche films rely less on stars and other expensive elements required for mainstream success. It may also result in more companies taking the approach of Todd Wagner's company 2929, which recently signed a deal with Steven Soderbergh to make six US$1 million films. Wagner argues that a key to keeping their budgets modest is to structure the concept of reward-for-success into their business model, and share revenue with their creative partners.

These linear films will increasingly have add-ons to extend the viewing experience—be they DVD or online. These are becoming more sophisticated, are often cross-platform, and have evolved to a point where they are no longer simply add-ons, but part of the project's conception. Evan Jones, creative director of Xenophile Media, recently outlined some innovative approaches to documentary, including branching narrative, the choose-your-own-adventure model; informed narrative, where the story changes according to the user's response (for example, 'show me this narrative from the perspective of a right-wing capitalist'); earned narrative, where the audience has to clear obstacles to get to the next part of the story; and telescopic narratives, where the detail of the story expands to reflect the degree of interest shown by the audience—for example, by finding hidden content.[55]

The paradigm change in content, however, is in the continued development of interactive programming, such as immersive role-playing worlds that develop online communities. While *SecondLife* is the highest-profile example, some of the projects currently being developed at the AFTRS' LAMP lab give some clues as to this sort of content. The *Abbey*, for example, uses a television series as a springboard for a more immersive experience, whereby 'users' enter and experience life in an abbey. *The Deep Sleep*, is a thirteen episode 5-minute weekly television and digital interactive television series as well as an immersive online world, in which the audience uncovers clues and solves a mystery. *In World*, by contrast, is a standalone show, broadcast live from inside a virtual world, which allows viewers to appear on television as their 3D avatars and submit mashed-up video, music, chat and games. Finally, *Urban Anarchy* is a cross-media exploration of urban art and street culture. Alongside short videos and documentaries the online element features a virtual city block, and the audience can contribute by submitting street art or creating art with the online tools.[56]

But which of these will be deemed worthy of government intervention in the future? Government has a set of criteria to determine the need for intervention:

there must, for example, be clear market failure, some level of demonstrated marketplace demand, and some determination regarding cultural significance. The latter question, in particular, is a highly subjective one, and the subject of ongoing contention. As Stuart Cunningham asks: What happens when the audience shifts away from one form of programming that has been deemed culturally important to one that has not? How do we measure whether a change—such as the move from 'authored texts to branded experiences'—is the result of corporate strategy or represents a generational, cultural shift?[57]

Once again this issue will play out as content forms develop in this new landscape. However, it is worth noting that the established forms of linear narrative have been tested over many years and through many platform changes. While in the long run the newer forms may prove to be no less culturally significant than the established art forms, they still have a case to make.

Future options

As we look to the options, it is important to keep in mind that while this new media landscape is opening up the conventional media world will continue to dominate. Furthermore, these broadcasters will still require access to spectrum, which will remain a valuable public resource. In other words, while strategies for future media need to be developed, broadcasting regulations will remain as relevant as ever and need to be modified and augmented.

The Australian Communications and Media

Authority (ACMA), for instance, could regulate terms of trade (in other words, set minimum licence fees) between producers and broadcasters, like the Office of Communications, the UK regulator. Ofcom's terms-of-trade regulations have had an incredible impact on the growth of the UK independent sector and the level of intellectual property retained by production companies. And new terms of trade were recently struck between producers and broadcasters, whereby negotiations for ancillary rights were separated and made subject to Ofcom. In other words, UK broadcasters cannot pursue a rights grab for all platforms.

ACMA has already set minimum licence fees for children's television, so there is some precedent. As broadcasters look to move across platforms there is a rationale to do it for other genres, to ensure that filmmakers can receive a fair share of the value generated by new media re-use. Similarly, ACMA could consider introducing an independent production quota, like the quota imposed on the BBC, in order to ensure a diversity of voices and ideas across new platforms.

Another way to address the terms of trade is more radical. Addressing the 2006 SPAA Conference, Harold Mitchell suggested pooling into a television production fund the hundreds of millions that the government earns from commercial broadcasters' annual licence payments. A variation might be to discount the licence payments to government in return for expenditure on Australian content. This could be linked not only to transmission hours, but to the prices or licence fees paid to producers, and could include a premium for the commissioning of programming from the independent sector.

Public broadcasters in this fragmenting media landscape are now more important than ever. As the BBC has shown, the new fragmenting digital world need not spell the end of public broadcasting, but might actually provide it with an entirely new sense of purpose. The BBC is now a world leader in innovation and content generation for the cross-platform environment.

The ABC is already a driver in the development of a content-rich online presence, particularly for audio, and has recently announced its cross-platform strategy for audio-visual content, which involves a greater engagement with the independent sector. Both the ABC and SBS will need to be further encouraged and resourced to provide a bridge between the conventional world of legacy media and the new multi-platform environment. In such an uncertain environment it is to the public broadcasters that we shall look to invest in quality programming, and to take the risk on innovation and experimentation in future narrative and interactive forms. This will require dedicated money for content as well as new platforms. It will also require a set of terms-of-trade guidelines, similar to those proposed for commercial broadcasters, to ensure that independents receive fair and equitable dealings on non-broadcast rights.

In short, Australian audiences should always know that if they are looking for original Australian content of quality—whether they want to access programs via broadcast or the net—that they can find it at the ABC or SBS. The public broadcasters should be seen, in an uncertain media landscape, as a home for quality Australian programming.

A content strategy for the digital age

What is most important, in the longer term, is to move beyond considerations of isolated policy initiatives and to begin developing an integrated strategy that considers everything from regulation to tax mechanisms, from the public broadcasters to professional training, with the focus always returning to Australian content.

I believe that government and industry need to stand back, take a long hard look at where the industry is likely to go over the next ten to twenty years, and start asking questions about the future place of content within it. Interventions such as this *Platform Paper* are just the start of a conversation that needs work, structure and rigour. How do we navigate this emerging media landscape? How can Australian films take advantage of these opportunities and challenges? What comprehensive set of strategies can we put in place to ensure Australian content remains a player, that audiences can continue to enjoy quality Australian content, and the industry can prosper?

For too long we have focused solely on production, looking for ways to make the best of a flawed system—hoping that if we just make better stuff then the audiences won't be able to resist us, that if we build it they will come. It is my firm view that only by re-examining the system in a holistic manner, moving beyond the silos that have dominated the debates, that we will devise the strategies needed for a viable production sector. The place of film needs to be considered in light of the entire value chain of production, from development through to exhibition, and strategic interventions made at every point.

This was the objective in 2005 of the Industry Strategic Plan proposal of the Australian Screen Council—the industry peak body formed by ASDA, the Screen Producers' Association of Australia, the Media Entertainment and Arts Alliance, and the Australian Writers' Guild. This plan was overtaken by the Federal Government's 2006 review of film support mechanisms, and so has not been a priority for them over the past nine months. However, as this review reaches its conclusion, now is the perfect opportunity to look more broadly at the future of the sector and for the industry and government to chart a path ahead for growth.

How do we address development? Are the current models working for conventional forms? What new programs and funding models are required to develop the content forms of tomorrow, and encourage creative practitioners to grasp the potential of cross-platform production? Do we need to broaden current practice to provide strategic interventions throughout the careers of creative practitioners, rather than just at the start? What is required to assist and lift the scale of Australian production? What are the best settings to attract and reward private investment? What are the impediments to production and what new methodologies can be developed to allow the industry to achieve creatively and commercially successful films?

Then there is distribution. What other mechanisms are required to ensure that films have the best opportunities of reaching audiences? What innovative approaches are there for distribution? Can incentives be built in to assist distributors of Australian films? Does specific funding need to be directed to marketing? And finally, how do we get better access to screens? What role can the AFC's laudable digital cinema network play in releasing Australian films outside the commercial theatres? How do we work through all the regulatory issues that I have outlined to ensure that Australian programs and films still have a place on Australian television and other platforms?

These are just some of the questions that need to be asked, and no-one has all of the answers yet. Together we must start navigating the hype curve by looking at the facts, asking the questions, and busting whatever myths we can. Most importantly, we need to start looking at the future at a macro level. Only by stepping back and looking at the structure as a whole do we stand any chance of developing the strategies that will create a sustainable and prosperous future for our industry.

Endnotes

1 'Where are we now?', *Screen International,* 1 September 2006, p. 6.
2 *The Long Tail* (New York: Random House, 2006), p. 127.
3 Quoted by Gubbins, p. 7.
4 *What Price a Creative Economy?,* Platform Paper No. 9 (Sydney: Currency House, 2006), p. 25.
5 One line of argument about Australian content in the 1970s suggested that diversity of quality content would only be achieved if we reduced the number of outlets: fewer programs would mean better programs.
6 'SPAA Conference, 2006', Urban Cinefile, at http://www.urbancinefile.com.au/home/view.asp?a=12520&s=Forum (accessed 17 February 2007).
7 'Evolve and Prosper: Finding Colleagues in a Complex World', NAB Convention, Broadcast Management Conference, Las Vegas, 25 April 2006.
8 Quoted in Jock Given, *Turning Off the Television* (Sydney: UNSW Press, 2003), p. 81.
9 Quoted in press release announcing PwC's *Global Entertainment and Media Outlook Report,* 2006–10.
10 'Australia's media future', *Media Report,* ABC-Radio National, 10 August 2006 at http://www.abc.net.au/rn/mediareport/stories/2006/1711568.htm (accessed 15 February 2007).
11 Some claim that the revolution began when BitTorrent became widespread. Mark Pesce, for example, argued that the key date was 18 October 2004, the day that episode '33' of *Battlestar Galactica* was shared globally peer-to-peer via BitTorrent prior to being screened in the USA.

12 'Where are we now?', p. 6.
13 Tom Wolzien, 'Harnessing the power of TV in a two-way world', Television Bureau of Advertising, Annual Marketing Conference, New York, 20 April 2006.
14 Brooks Barnes, 'Big TV's broadband blitz', *Wall Street Journal,* 1 August 2006.
15 'Moving movies from DVD to digital?', *Screen Digest,* 1 October 2006.
16 Quoted by Gubbins, p. 7.
17 Quoted by Lara Sinclair, 'Free-to-air copping a download', *Australian,* 14 December 2006.
18 http://cryptome.org/hrcw-hear.htm (accessed 20 February 2007).
19 For example, Anderson argues that the advent of the internet means that economics debates will need now to be reframed, within the context of abundance rather than scarcity.
20 *The Long Tail,* p. 18.
21 *Media Report,* ABC-Radio National, 10 August 2006.
22 http://www.netvideo.dreamhosters.com/MarkPesce261105.mov (accessed 20 February 2007).
23 *Turning Off the Television,* p. 214.
24 *The Long Tail,* p. 65.
25 Quoted by Simon Canning, *Australian,* Media, 8 February 2007.
26 *The Long Tail,* p. 193.
27 For example, the 2006 thriller, *Snakes on a Plane,* was developed as a form of marketing, soliciting ideas and scenarios from an internet audience during the scriptwriting process.
28 Further discussion, see http://www.Screenhub,com.au/ (accessed 17 February 2007).
29 *Screen International,* 1 September 2006.

30 *Media Report*, 10 August 2006.
31 *Wall Street Journal*, 3 August 2006.
32 *Wall Street Journal*, 2 September 2006.
33 *Wall Street Journal*, 3 August 2006.
34 *Australian*, Media, 8 February 2007.
35 *Variety*, 10 September 2006.
36 See Lara Sinclair, *Australian*, Media, 1 February 2007.
37 http://www.screenhub.com.au/news/shownewsarticle.asp?news (accessed 17 February 2007).
38 Quoted by Mark Pesce, http://www.netvideo.dream-hosters.com/MarkPesce261105.mov (accessed 20 February 2007).
39 *UK TV Content in the Digital Age: Opportunities and Challenges*, A Report by Oliver and Ohlbaum Associates Ltd for PACT, January 2006, p 3.
40 '*Media Report*, ABC-Radio National, 10 August 2006.
41 Jock Given, *Turning off the Television* (Sydney: UNSW Press, 2003), p. 217.
42 *The Future Environment facing the Canadian Broadcasting System: Comments to the CRTC by the Coalition of Canadian Audio-Visual Unions*, 1 September 2006.
43 'Plugging the Web into TV', *Wall Street Journal*, 4 August 2006.
44 'Sticking to the Tube', *Variety*, 9 September 2006.
45 *The Future of Television in Canada*, Green Paper, 8 June 2006. Noam estimated that if 1% of European households ordered a program, say *Desperate Housewives*, it would use up all the backbone capacity originally installed in the 1990s.
46 'The Future of Television', Keynote Address, ASDA Conference, 2006.
47 The figures in this paragraph are taken from the AFC analysis of MPDAA data, *Get the Picture*, at www.

afc.gov.au/gtp/wcboshare.html (accessed 19 February 2007).

48 *Los Angeles Times*, 16 August 2006.

49 'Free-to-air copping a download', p. 17.

50 Quoted by Brooks Barnes, *Wall Street Journal*, 1 August 2006.

51 'Wagner and Cuban's 2929 Entertainment pacts with Steven Soderbergh', at http://www.hd.net/pressrelease.html?2005-04-29-01.html (accessed 21 February 2007).

52 At the Oxford Business Alumni Forum, Sydney, 23 November 2006. See http://www.oba.com.au/ (accessed 22 February 2007).

53 *ACMAsphere*, no. 15 (December 2006), p. 17.

54 *The Long Tail*, p. 198.

55 'Storytelling in a Cross-Media World', *ScreenHub*, 17 November 2006.

56 http://www.lamp.edu.au (accessed 19 February 2007).

57 *What Price a Creative Economy?*, p. 25.

Readers' Forum

Michael Richards is author of *Grow the Arts, Reap the Harvest*, and was lead writer on Arts Queensland's 2005 Regional Arts Development Fund evaluation.

The great strength of Lyndon Terracini's paper is that it has emerged from his own personal odyssey through the arts and is enriched by his responses and insights into performances and events he has variously instigated and participated in. Lyndon has, in the vernacular (appropriate given his concern for popular engagement) 'been there and done that'. He knows what he is talking about, and he speaks not with the studied detachment and supposed objectivity of the scholar, but with the visceral conviction and innate authority of the partisan. Much of what he advocates is important and highly prescient, and warrants implementation or support.

Lyndon's call for 'a regional state of mind' amounts to an appeal—and I interpret his argument in my own terms, at the risk of extending it slightly—for arts production to be decentralised, democratised and reintegrated into everyday life. For this to happen the arts must stimulate, foster and contribute to a living dialogue that permeates communities and engages their people by ventilating issues of real and immediate concern, through familiar and meaningful voices and iconographies.

Lyndon articulates his call primarily in terms of regionalism and place, but in our shared lexicon, regionalism and place are about far more than geography and location; they embrace all the material and immaterial contexts, characteristics and accoutrements of the human condition, such as both physical and intangible environments, beliefs, values and attitudes, vocations, aspiration and fears, and so on.

Truly relevant and meaningful art will thus reflect a strong awareness of its 'place' of genesis, and become a celebration of the culture and people of that place, resonating with and expressing a sense of their community. Indeed, the rediscovery and strengthening of community is a necessary accompaniment to the creation of such art. The joint processes of creating art and asserting community intertwine and reinforce each other, reintegrating the arts into the fabric of daily life, and fostering not only more relevant and powerful art, but more satisfying and creative lives.

This leads to what I call a 'creative community culture'. Such a culture discredits the spurious nexus between consumption and lifestyle, and allows people to live richer and more satisfying lives without increasing their consumption of material goods. A necessary characteristic is that people understand and are empowered to tell their own stories in their own voices, as an antidote to the repressive and stultifying uniformity of globally franchised culture.

Other principles Lyndon advocates are equally important. His call for arts funding to be seen in terms of research and investment is seminal and goes to the heart of arts funding policy. It mandates the corollary that we should be prepared to drill many 'dry wells' in order to discover one that is productive, and it requires that we recognise and accept diverse and oblique channels of investment return. I whole-heartedly endorse it.

Perhaps the most important aspect of this call for a return to relevance for the arts is that they should draw attention to and expose for discussion critical issues of public concern (moral, social and environmental). The arts provide versatile tools, both delicate and powerful, to help us analyse, consider and comment upon these issues that confront us all—from drugs, violence, family breakdown and social dislocation to the sustainable use or resources and the looming catastrophe of global warming.

In this respect, although Lyndon does not discuss it, the arts have a key contribution to make to the health and effectiveness of our democracy, by amplifying grass-roots concerns and providing diverse channels of communication and feedback, adding to those essential arteries that carry the lifeblood of civil society.

I am less comfortable with Lyndon's use of the pyramid as a metaphor for his ideal cultural configuration. The pyramid is inherently hierarchical and inflexible, and it provides the quintessential structure of the arts bureaucracies Lyndon decries. As such, it sits uncomfortably with his call for popular engagement and creative management. The pyramid also suggests, inevitably to me, a vertical scale of quality and value in which both are equated with altitude, and so fosters notions of elitism and exclusivity which are at odds with Lyndon's general egalitarian and democratic thrust.

In fact, we already have a pyramid; it is the structure of our society, a pyramid of prestige, money and power. Even at its most benign, this pyramid is oligarchic and elitist; at its most pernicious it becomes oppressive and autocratic. If the arts are to be more egalitarian and further the democratic cause, our aim should be, if not to demolish this pyramid, then at least to flatten it by simultaneously reducing its height and broadening its base, and by creating more numerous, shorter and less constricted connections between its apex and its base.

Antonietta Morgillo is a writer, performer and theatre maker. She currently works as the Program Officer for the Theatre Board of the Australia Council.

There are lots of issues that could be raised when addressing the making of art in a regional environment: what works in the country, what do people want in the country and what the difficulties, both financial and otherwise, are. And many of these were raised during the panel discussion of Lyndon Terracini's paper in Albury in February 2007. However, rather than focusing on the challenges, let's focus on the inspirational aspects of Lyndon's paper.

The projects Lyndon describes use a diversity of strategies to raise substantial funds, make great work, and engage effectively with the community. These projects offer ample evidence that there are new, and successful, ways of making theatre in a regional environment. It's not easy, and there are many complications, but there are also many possibilities.

We—that is, theatre makers, producers, funding bodies—are all looking at ways to generate sustainable theatre-making in a regional environment. Finding a model, however, that will create innovative, high-quality work that engages its audience, whether or not that work tells stories of the place in which it was created, is a bit of an experiment in the current climate. We, at the Theatre Board, have been encouraging some of these experiments by cooking up initiatives that provide would-be theatre makers with opportunities.

Our Touring the Theatre Making Process initiative supported partnerships between professional theatre artists and regional communities to create new work. The idea was that artists who had a tried and tested process would choose a community that would welcome their residency and be willing to make a theatre work with them.

This initiative contributed funding to Big hART's 'Gold' project, Y Space's 'La Trobe City Proposal' and Darwin Theatre Company's work 'The Road to Minyerri'. In this last project, a new work was created with the isolated Aboriginal community of Minyerri near Roper River, 600km south of Darwin. The elders now see the project, for which the entire community collaborated in transforming a rock outcrop into an amphitheatre for the performance, as a way for their language and local stories to regain importance in the eyes of younger people in their community. They are keen to repeat the exercise next year.

Local Stages is another Theatre Board initiative, in partnership with Arts NSW, that aims to encourage regional performing arts centres (PACs) to move from being predominantly presenters of touring work, to becoming hubs for local theatre-making. The idea of this experiment is to make more effective use of the existing cultural infrastructure in regional areas, unlocking the potential of these PACs, and promoting ownership of such activity by local governments, and through this, to help local artists make great work in a supported environment.

There is now a creative producer in each of three PACs in NSW: Anne-Louise Rentell in Wollongong, Margie Breen in Bathurst and Scott Howie in Griffith. Their role is to create programs that nurture professional practice in their region. They have been given a budget and resources to enable them to commission and produce new work by local artists. Local Stages has also been launched in regional South Australia in partnership with Arts SA and Country Arts SA. The creative producer, Stephen Mayhew, is located at Country Arts SA, and he will be focusing on two regions, the Upper Spencer Gulf and the Lower South East, areas that include the towns of Port Augusta and Mount Gambier respectively.

Local Stages will give performing artists in regional areas significantly greater access to resources and facilities, and thus relieve them of the burden of having to create and maintain their own companies. And Australian culture will be enriched, as it has been by Lyndon's remarkable work, by the creation of innovative works in other regional areas.

Of course, there are challenges working in the regions, but then artists trying to survive in the high-rent cities are also under pressure. I call on those with the creative minds and the years of experience in making theatre to help devise more innovative, strategic ways of connecting people, organisations, infrastructure, and funding sources so as to enable artists to keep making high quality art in, and from every part of our country. There are many possible experiments that haven't even been envisioned yet. Let Lyndon Terracini's work in Queensland point the way.